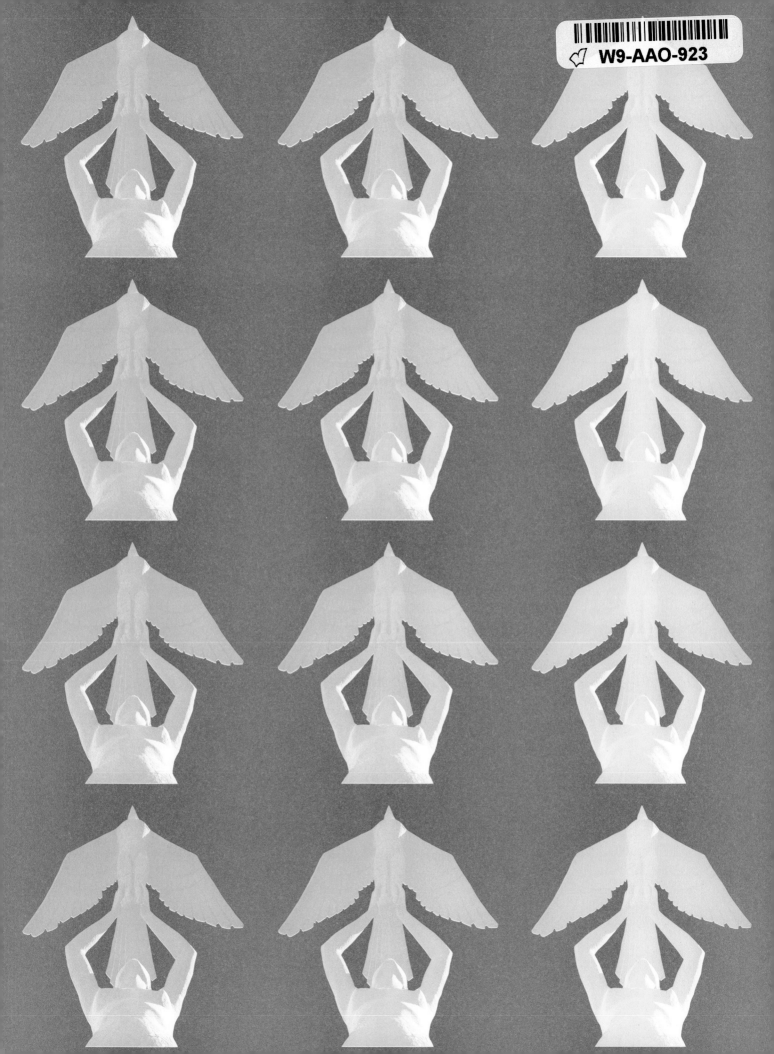

ATLANTA

a brave and beautiful city

ATLANTA

a brave and beautiful city

PHOTOGRAPHS BY PETER BENEY

INTRODUCTION BY CELESTINE SIBLEY

Peachtree Publishers, Ltd.

Published by
PEACHTREE PUBLISHERS, LTD.
494 Armour Circle, N.E.
Atlanta, Georgia 30324

Photographs copyright © 1986 Peter Beney

Introduction copyright © 1986 Celestine Sibley

Manufactured in Japan

First printing

Library of Congress Catalog Card Number 86-61544

ISBN 0-934601-03-8

Design by Paulette L. Lambert

ACKNOWLEDGMENTS

We wish to thank the following persons and organizations for their generous assistance:

The Alliance Theatre Company and production staff of Sandra Deer's adaptation of Charles Dickens's novel *Great Expectations*, including Fred Chappell, director; Charles Caldwell, set designer; and Marilyn Rennagel, lighting designer;

The Atlanta Ballet production of *The Nutcracker*, music by Peter Tchaikovsky, choreography by George Ballanchine;

The Atlanta Hawks and photographer Scott Cunningham;

The management and photography staff of the Atlanta *Journal & Constitution*;

The Atlanta Shakespeare Company, cast and crew of William Shakespeare's *A Midsummer Night's Dream*, director Jeffrey Watkins and Manuel's Tavern owners Manuel and Robert Maloof;

Centers for Disease Control;

The Dekalb County School System and Fernbank Science Center;

Georgia-Pacific Corporation;

The High Museum of Art for permission to photograph *The Shade* by Auguste Rodin (French, 1840-1917) — 1968 cast in bronze from the original mold by the Susse Foundry, Paris; commissioned by the Musée Rodin. Gift of the French government to the Atlanta Arts Alliance, 1968;

Moakler Photographic Services Incorporated for their careful E6 processing of the film for this book;

The cast and crew of *Lust Into Small Change*, by Lee Heuermann, a cabaret at Nexus Theater, including Rodger French and Walter Limehouse;

First Sergeant A.G. Scott and the U.S. Army Signal Corps Band of Fort Gordon, Georgia;

Architect Rick Sibly for permission to photograph his home designs.

PHOTO CREDITS

Atlanta Falcons photo by Joey Ivansco; Atlanta Golf Classic photo provided by Georgia-Pacific Corporation; Atlanta Hawks photo by Scott Cunningham; Atlanta Journal 500 photo by Rich Addicks; Atlanta Steeplechase photo by Nick Arroyo; Atlanta Symphony photo by Chipp Jamison; Ballet photo provided by the Atlanta Ballet; CDC photo provided by the Centers for Disease Control; Georgia Tech football photo and Peachtree Road Race aerial shot by Calvin Cruce; Peachtree Road Race spectators photo by Billy Downs.

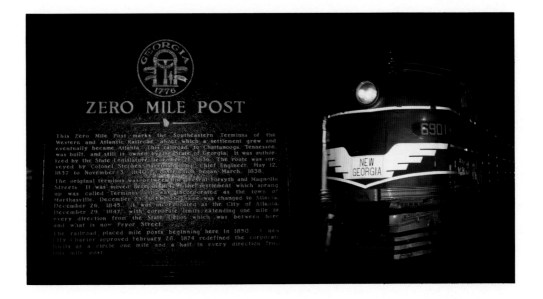

INTRODUCTION

Henry W. Grady said it first.

Back in 1886, the young editor of the *Atlanta Constitution* went to New York to address the New England Society. Bent on healing the wounds of the Civil War (he was credited with "loving a nation back to peace"), he had a message, he said, for General William T. Sherman, "an able man — though kind of careless with fire."

The message: "From the ashes he left us in 1864, we have raised a brave and beautiful city that somehow or other caught the sunshine in the bricks and mortar of our homes, and have builded therein not one ignoble prejudice or memory."

Now a hundred years later, celebrated photographer Peter Beney has been inspired by that message.

"A brave and beautiful city," he quotes. "I like that. I want to capture that in my pictures. Atlanta — brave and beautiful city."

This book, the fifteenth Peter Beney has filled with pictures of some of the most handsome and interesting cities of the world, achieves that spectacularly.

The little city of which Henry Grady was so proud was burgeoning, no doubt about it. Seven thousand people had voted in its last municipal election. It had attracted to its still somewhat sooty center a grand total of 303 business enterprises with an impressive payroll of more than two million dollars. And a Confederate veteran named John Pemberton was tinkering with a formula for what he hoped would be "a palatable syrup," soon to be called Coca-Cola.

Atlanta was on her way.

The phoenix bird of Egyptian mythology, which, burned to ashes, rose again in renewed youth and beauty, was flapping its wings. People of the little town had heard about something they were determined to create for themselves. A diarist of the day called it "the good life."

Today Peter Beney, camera in hand, focusing on a city that reaches out into fifteen counties with a population running into millions, records that Atlanta has achieved not only "the good life" but what many of its sons and daughters consider the *best* life.

A visitor in 1848 recorded in his journal that he had never seen "more beauty than there was in the springtime in the groves all over Atlanta." He waxed poetic about the "lavish luxuriance"

of flowering plants, great trees and crystal streams, and then he said it again: "I have seen few things so fair in this world of beauty as were the Atlanta woods in 1848."

Atlanta's woods have receded somewhat before the march of building and growing, but the reverence for beauty abides. Atlantans liked that view of their town in 1848 and they ardently cherish it today. In the midst of spreading out in all directions with its subdivisions and office complexes, and reaching upward with its skyscrapers and the second busiest airport in the world, Atlanta is dotty about its trees and gardens.

It stages annual festivals to celebrate the glory of the dogwood, which trims its streets with a ruching of starchy white and delicate strawberry pink lace in the spring. It fights to preserve its old trees with city ordinances and vigilant citizens groups, and it constantly plants new trees — along the sidewalks and roadways, in concrete boxes downtown, anywhere there is a patch of hospitable earth.

Before the usually benign winter has passed, garden tours and flower shows have started. Camellias are blooming and azaleas girding up for that most flamboyant of early spring carnivals of color. Tulips are on the way, iris and roses follow, and the bounty of summer flowers fills humble dooryards and the grounds of great estates. Even after the tawny tide of chrysanthemum color has subsided in the fall,

Atlantans are thinking or planning or dreaming of gardening. They study it in classes at the Atlanta Botanical Garden or in Piedmont Park. They take horticulture courses at Emory University or travel to Athens to the University of Georgia's world-famous school of landscape design to learn serious things about drainage and grading of gardens.

The natural beauty of the foothills of the Blue Ridge mountains was Atlanta's legacy at birth. But catching the sunshine in the brick and mortar of its buildings, as Henry Grady put it, was another matter. In the antebellum Southern colonial mansions which Sherman missed — and there are enough of these still around to be seen in home and garden tours — the openness to the out-of-doors was there. Long galleries and balconies were traditional, and floor-to-ceiling windows invited light and air. The celebrated Neel Reid, whose mansions are cherished as showplaces among the estates of the north side and the splendid homes of Druid Hills, was the first of many architects to bring light and grace and symmetry to the brick and mortar of Atlanta homes and public buildings.

Two of the most public buildings contributing to the "good life" spell out the story in contemporary lines and planes. The big downtown public library designed by France's Marcel Breuer was the first, the six-level Robert W. Woodruff Arts Center is the newest. These structures not only draw from afar vistors interested in their physical beauty, but they nurture Atlantans culturally. The arts center, named for the man who ran John Pemberton's "palatable syrup" into a world-wide empire and gave more than $28 million to arts in the area, includes the High Museum of Art, the Atlanta Symphony Orchestra, the Alliance Theatre, the Atlanta Children's Theatre and the Atlanta College of Art.

There are Atlantans whose taste in architecture runs to the lively design of the big Atlanta-Fulton County Stadium, home of the baseball Braves and football Falcons, the $17-million Omni Coliseum, home of the Atlanta Hawks (basketball), or to Georgia Tech's famous Alexander Coliseum.

There's an old story, most certainly apocryphal, that back when Atlanta had a dearth of good restaurants and only a few notable hotels, some well-to-do citizen excused it by saying, "What do we need with restaurants and hotels? If a gentleman comes to town, he is welcome in our homes. If he isn't a gentleman, he isn't welcome at all."

That attitude, if in truth it existed, has long since vanished. Atlantans rejoice in a thriving tourist business and are pleased to offer variety and splendor in such landmark hotels as John Portman's original Hyatt Regency and the seventy-six-story mirrored tower, the Peachtree Plaza. And whether the visitors are domestic or from foreign lands, they have no trouble finding cuisine to suit them.

The visitor in 1848 was impressed by Atlanta's "crystal" water, much of it contained in the storied Chattahoochee river which curves around the city on its way to the Gulf of Mexico. That water has been put to maximum use, not only for drinking but for recreation as well, entrapped in two tremendous lakes north of the city where it offers sites for weekend and vacation homes and all the water sports. (An inland city, Atlanta claims one of the biggest yacht clubs in America.) The river itself, still beautiful despite the bridges that crisscross it and the apartments and homes which overlook parts of it, is also handy for rafting, canoeing, fishing and camping. There are ski resorts in the mountains within an easy drive of Atlanta and more than thirty golf courses in the area. One of these, the Atlanta Athletic Club, home club of famed grand-slammer Bobby Jones, has hosted the U.S. Open in years past.

Henry Grady wasn't into golf, of course. But he would have seen the wisdom in building so many of these richly rolling acres of green. After all, there's Atlanta's incomparable weather — an estimated 225 "good golfing days" a year.

Peter Beney, who insists he "only photographs the beautiful, never the ugly or depressing," found plenty for his camera to do in Atlanta, recording here examples of the vitality, the "sunshine," the energy and aliveness.

Henry Grady would be very proud.

Celestine Sibley

(Left) Lobby Georgia-Pacific Building

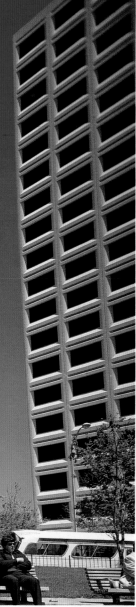

City scenes — Mounted police officers in Central City Park, a popular noontime gathering place

Georgia's State Capitol, completed in 1889; the capitol dome is covered with gold leaf mined in Dahlonega, Georgia

Following pages: Arts and entertainment come alive in Atlanta — (left to right) The Limelight, one of the city's hottest nightspots; The Fox Theatre (1929), a registered national landmark; Cabaret at Nexus Theater; The Atlanta Shakespeare Company at Manuel's Tavern

Atlanta is a central point for Southeastern transport

Scenes from Atlanta's Hyatt Regency
Hotel, designed by architect John
Portman, and (far right) the historic
Candler Building's intricately sculpted
marble staircase

Atlanta's annual Dogwood festival — complete with a colorful hot-air balloon race — celebrates the rejuvenating beauty of springtime in the city

A breath of spring at the Atlanta Botanical
Garden: (top left) the James M. Cox Courtyard
of the Gardenhouse, (above) the Japanese
Garden

The Varsity, the world's largest drive-in restaurant

The Plaza Shopping Center (top) and St.
Charles Deli of the Virginia-Highlands
neighborhood

Colony Square Hotel, a shopping, dining and business complex, and (bottom right) the nearby AT&T building

Ansley Park's stately homes and (left)
the Robert W. Woodruff Arts Center,
Home of the Atlanta Symphony
Orchestra and the Alliance Theatre

Following pages: The Galleria of the Woodruff Arts Center

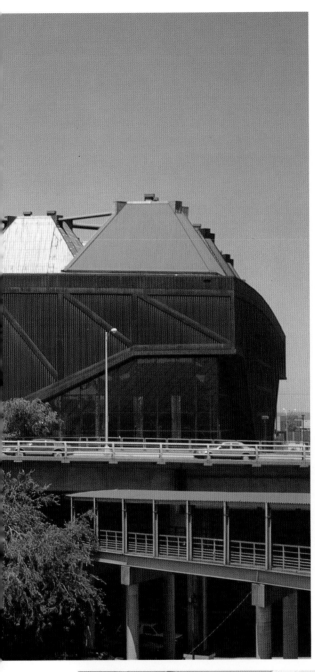

The impressive Omni complex includes (left) the Omni Coliseum, (below left) the Omni International Hotel and its shopping mall, and (below right) the World Congress Center

Atlanta's vibrant news community: The Atlanta *Journal & Constitution* features new high speed offset presses capable of producing 75,000 copies each per hour. At right are the studios of WXIA Channel 11 and WSB Radio

Scenes from the Martin Luther King, Jr., National Historic Site.
Above is the parlor of the King birth home (1895). (Facing page,
top) The sanctuary of Ebenezer Baptist Church; at right, the
Freedom Hall Complex

Following pages: Bedroom of King birth home

Morehouse College, founded in 1867, and the Morehouse School of Medicine

Georgia State University, founded in 1913

Clockwise from top left: the distinctive columns of the Federal Reserve Building,
a colorful outdoor market at Five Points and the First National Bank building.
Above are the row houses of Baltimore Place

Georgia Institute of Technology, founded in 1885. At right is Fort McPherson, the first permanent post of the U.S. Army in the Southeast

The Wren's Nest, home of Joel Chandler Harris. The author of the Uncle Remus stories lived at this Atlanta address (now a national historic landmark) from 1881 until his death in 1908

A few of the city's most popular residents at Zoo Atlanta in
Grant Park

Atlanta's renowned Cyclorama and Civil War Museum; the painting, a re-creation of the Battle of Atlanta fought July 22, 1864, is 42 feet tall and 358 feet long

The historic Herndon Home, built in 1910 by former slave turned businessman Alonzo Franklin Herndon, is in the Beaux Arts style and is listed in the National Register of Historic Places

Oakland, Atlanta's oldest
cemetery (1850), the burial site of
Margaret Mitchell, Bobby Jones,
twenty-three mayors of Atlanta
and six Georgia governors

The colors of Cabbagetown, the old mill village of the now-defunct Fulton Bag and Cotton Mill

A private garden in southeast Atlanta

The elegant beauty of Druid Hills, designed by
Frederick Law Olmsted

Druid Hills

Agnes Scott College, founded in 1889

The hospital and President's home at Emory University,
founded in 1836

Following pages: Emory University's Pitts Theology Library, at 400,000
volumes is the second largest theological library
in North America

Emory University Museum of Art and Archaeology

In Dekalb County: (top left) the Old Dekalb County
Courthouse, (bottom) the Centers for Disease Control

Georgia's Stone Mountain Park, featuring the largest exposed granite rock in the world. The carved figures on the face of the mountain are (left to right) Confederate President Jefferson Davis, General Robert E. Lee and General Thomas "Stonewall" Jackson

Inman park, one of Atlanta's first suburbs, exudes Victorian charm. At far right is Callan Castle, former home of business leader and philanthropist Asa Candler, built in 1903 in the Beaux Arts style

Inman Park

Some of the unique offerings of the museum, classroom and woodland complex at the Fernbank Science Center. Fernbank's Observatory features the largest telescope in the world used principally for public education and a magnificent planetarium

Following pages: Breathtaking Cator Woolford Gardens in full bloom

Autumn at Morningside's Orme Park and (left) Morningside Baptist
Church

Following pages: Callanwolde Fine Arts Center

In-town living with a contemporary flair

The Atlanta Historical Society's 1920s Italianate villa, the Swan House (left), featuring an elaborately elegant dining room (right), along with the 1840 plantation-style Tullie Smith House (below right) and log cabin (bottom right)

Following pages: The Swan House's grand lobby staircase

The Swan Coach House Art Gallery (above)
and Restaurant (bottom right), also on the
grounds of the Atlanta Historical Society

These and following pages: The opulent elegance of the Georgia Governor's Mansion

Preceding page: A Garden in Buckhead

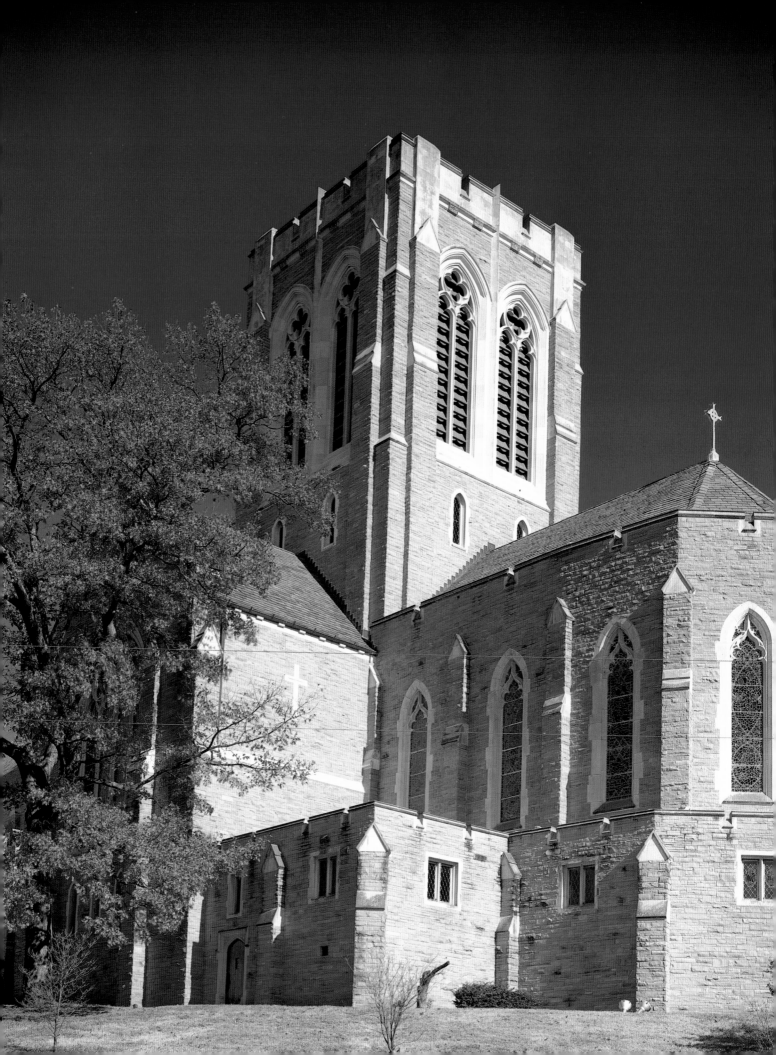

Atlanta's beautiful churches: (clockwise from below) Christ The King Cathedral, Rock Spring Presbyterian Church, The Temple, Second Ponce De Leon Baptist Church, (facing page) The Cathedral of St. Philip

The distinctive grace of Buckhead homes

Following pages: A Buckhead home in springtime;
Anthony's Restaurant

Along the Chattahoochee River National
Recreation Area; Above is Morgan Falls Dam

Chattahoochee River views

Shopping and dining at Lenox Square and Perimeter Mall

Springtime sights at the Waverly Hotel and its connecting shopping center the Galleria include the Jubilee Arts Festival (top left)

The bell tower at Oglethorpe University, founded in 1835

The nautical appointments of Dante's Down The Hatch restaurant

The suburban showplaces of North Fulton and Gwinnett

Reminders of our heritage in Cobb County: At right is Ruff's Mill, a battle site of July, 1864; (Facing page, bottom) Fort Peach Tree, built in 1814 at the mouth of Peachtree Creek

The past meets the present in Marietta: Above is the First Baptist Church; (facing page, top left) the twenty-three-acre Marietta National Cemetery was established in 1866. Its 17,000 gravesites include soldiers from the Revolutionary War

Historic Roswell: Above is the Roswell Presbyterian Church (1840)

Above is Bulloch Hall, built in 1840 in the Greek Revival style.
At right is the Primrose Cottage fence, built of hand-turned Rosemary
Pine. Roswell Mill entertainment complex is at left

Atlanta performing arts: (below) the Atlanta Symphony; (top right) the Atlanta Ballet; (bottom right) the Alliance Theatre auditorium

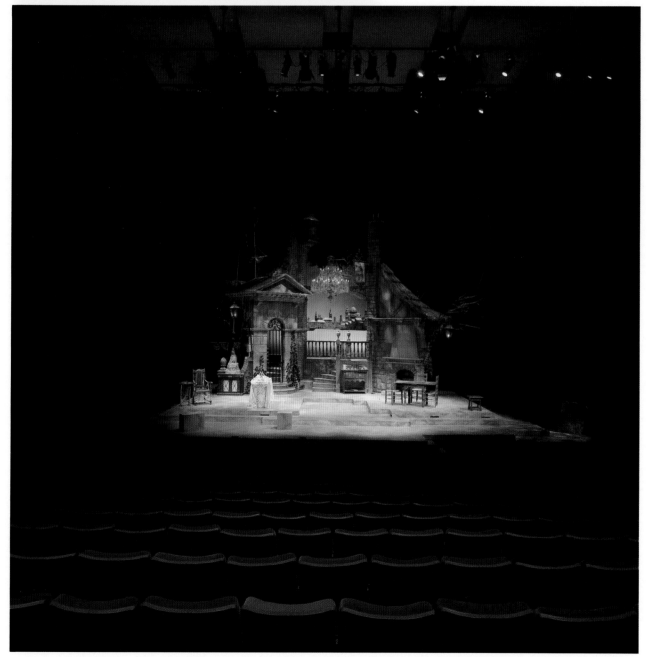

Atlanta's thriving business community: Coca-Cola, the city's favorite beverage

Above is the satellite dish garden at Turner Broadcasting System;
right and below is one of North Fulton's modern office complexes

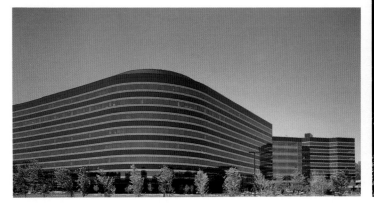

From any direction Atlanta's majestic skyline is a welcoming sight; Above is the Atlanta-Fulton County Stadium, home of the Braves and Falcons

Atlanta's love affair with sports
thrives on the Braves and Falcons
at Atlanta-Fulton County
Stadium, the Peachtree Road
Race, the Atlanta *Journal* 500 at
Atlanta International Raceway,
tennis at the Bryan "Bitsy" Grant
Tennis Center and Georgia Tech
football at Grant Field

The Atlanta Steeplechase, Georgia-Pacific Atlanta Golf Classic and Atlanta Hawks basketball at the Omni

Six Flags Over Georgia

The splendor of Atlanta's hotels: the Marriott Marquis . . .

... the Westin Peachtree
Plaza (above and top), the
Atlanta Hilton (far right)
and Colony Square Hotel

High rise: (top) the Georgia Power Building, (left)
Peachtree Plaza, (right) the Flatiron Building (1897) and
(facing page) Central City Park

Downtown shapes and colors; the statue at near left is of Robert W. Woodruff

Urban landscapes: (clockwise from above) Central City Park, Fulton County Courthouse (1914), and the old Georgia Depot at Underground Atlanta

Atlanta is served by a sophisticated
transportation network

Cityscapes: In background at right is the Shrine of the Immaculate Conception (1847)

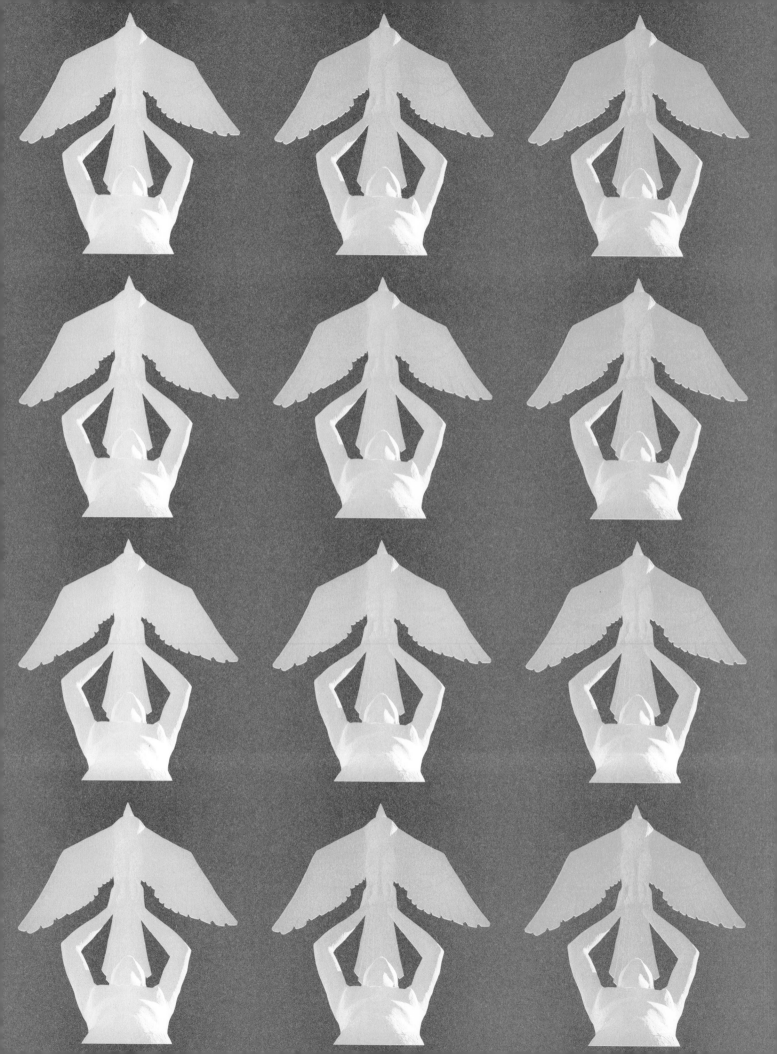